COLORADO
SCENIC WILDFLOWERS

Roger Edrinn
Photographs and Text

Front cover: *A mountainside dominated by **rosy paintbrush** with **blue lupine** and **subalpine arnica** in the Maroon Bells–Snowmass Wilderness.*

Page 1: *A symphony of wildflowers sings its morning song on a steep hillside. Members of the choir include **columbine**, **silvery lupine**, **Wyoming paintbrush**, and **heartleaf arnica**.*

Page 2: *First light caresses the sculpted ridges of Treasury Mountain while a lush carpet of **rosy paintbrush**, **alpine arnica** and **white geranium** await the morning sun.*

Title page: *A pastel patch of **Colorado tansy aster** bask in warm morning light in the Pike National Forest.*

Back cover: *A delightful clutch of **Colorado columbine** near Lily Lake in the Sangre de Cristo Range.*

Photographs and Text Copyright © 1997
Roger Edrinn

Published by: Above the Timber
2366 Wapiti Road
Fort Collins, CO 80525-3512

ISBN 1-881059-33-2

Printed in Singapore

For the latest product information, expanded descriptions, color photos, current address, order forms, and much more visit Above the Timber on the Internet.

www.AboveTheTimber.com

Additional products with altitude from Above the Timber featuring internationally acclaimed photographer Roger Edrinn:

Books:
Fourteeners–A Photo Journey
Colorado–Scenic Splendor
Colorado–Mountain Reflections
Colorado–Autumn Splendor

CALENDARS:
Fourteeners
Colorado–Scenic Splendor

POSTERS:
Fourteeners II (photo collage)
Wildflowers (photo collage)
Maroon Bells – Autumn
Maroon Bells – Winter
Longs Peak – Diamond
Mount of the Holy Cross

Foreword

Thank you for selecting *Scenic Wildflowers*, a celebration of Colorado's magnificent wildflowers in their natural setting. Through a unique combination of circumstances—geographic location, elevation variation, and weather—Colorado has the most glorious mixture of flowers and mountains in America. A major aspect of this uniqueness can be attributed to the tendency for the most spectacular flower displays to happen near timberline. Colorado has more area at timberline than any of the 48 contiguous states, enhancing the opportunity for breathtaking flowers.

My passion is to create dramatic photographs of flowers, mountains and light, as if you were there standing in my shoes. I want the reader to sense my joy as I was taking these images. The photographs are from a multi-year effort, with the goal of creating the best book ever about scenic wildflowers.

Photo selection was not based on showing every flower species. Inasmuch as there are hundreds upon hundreds of named flowers, it would be impossible to show them all in a 72-page book. The emphasis is on the beauty of the flowers and incorporating them as the major element of each scene with photographic excellence.

While not intended as a flower identification book, I believe you will find

*The incredible scarlet-red of the **claret cup cactus** contrasts with its prickly exterior.*

many of the flowers easier to identify in this book than any other by virtue of their context. While there are many flower identification books, most emphasize tight photos, often in less than ideal light, making it impossible to understand where the flower grows. To me, the question of where a flower grows is often as interesting as the flower itself.

Flower identification is a hair-pulling experience, with many nearly identical subspecies to distinguish between. I've concluded that the plant characteristics (leaf shape, size, connection to the stem, etc.) are as important as the flower in making a determination. I have many flower books and I pored over them in an effort to correctly identify each flower. If I've erred, please enjoy the photographs and drop me a note so I can do better in the future.

For those of you who wish to create your own flower photos, I've devoted two pages at the end of the book to a discussion of flower photography, with a particular emphasis on the quality of light.

Roger Edrinn

Overleaf: ***Arrowleaf senecio*** *grows tall and dense along Trap Creek, Neota Wilderness, north of Rocky Mountain National Park.*

*S*mall pools and lakes, high in the alpine domain, add to the mountain experience. **Marsh marigold** thrive in the cold wet conditions above 12,000 feet, where it is common for these pools to freeze overnight. The delightful patterns on the frozen surface break up the sunrise reflection from the distant San Juan Mountains. A month later, **sunloving aster**, **bistort**, and **alpine avens** flourish above one of the Yule Lakes in the Raggeds Wilderness.

$\mathcal{T}$he lush greens of the Maroon Bells–Snowmass Wilderness add a delicious richness to mountain flower photographs. At the south end of the wilderness, **elephant heads** stand tall in the evening light. To the right, **tall chiming bells** and Maroon Bells ring in the morning.

The desert-like conditions of the Great Sand Dunes National Monument highlight a single wind-blown **sunflower**, which contrasts with the multitude of flowers present on a high mesa in Dinosaur National Monument.

$\mathcal{F}$og-shrouded mountains with light rain make for great flower photo conditions. All winter long, avalanches roar down into American Basin, the origin of the Lake Fork of the Gunnison River, filling the valley to great depths. Frequently the flowers cannot wait for the snow to melt before blooming. This cliffside flower garden contains **alpine sunflower**, **king's crown**, and **alpine forget-me-not**. The other foggy scene shows lush **Parry primrose** and **marsh marigold** south of Animas Forks in the San Juan Mountains.

*H*azy-bright conditions provide the best light for flower photography, notice the definition and fine detail in the flower petals. **Pink lupine**, **silvery lupine**, and **common dandelion** share a lush meadow below the Medicine Bow Mountains in North Park. Silvery lupine are very common in Colorado, pink lupine are extremely rare. The massive red sandstone formations typical of Colorado National Monument, support **purple penstemon**, **Indian paintbrush** and **white loco** above a steep cliff.

Overleaf: Part of a 100-acre field of **Colorado columbine** in the mountains west of Silverton. Winter avalanches clear trees from the slopes creating perfect conditions for the sun-loving columbine. The flowers were defended by Kamikaze mosquitoes, be prepared to give blood!

*pring flowers, which cannot wait for the snow to melt, are an especially bright reminder that summer is just ahead. **Mule's ears** are common on sagebrush-covered hillsides between 6,000 and 9,000 feet in May and June. By contrast, **avalanche lilies** are seldom found that low. The distant snowcapped mountains behind the mule's ears are in the Gore Range and the avalanche lilies were photographed on Rabbit Ears Pass near Steamboat Springs.

*E*arly morning, before the sun strikes the ground, is a good time to photograph flowers. **Rosy paintbrush** and **mountain candytuft** decorate a small clearing above Hancock in the Sawatch Range. Similarly, **blue columbine**, **mountain bluebell**, **lemon paintbrush**, and **bistort** grow in profusion in Horseshoe Basin, Front Range.

$\mathcal{A}$lpine lakes are a magnet for beautiful wildflowers. **Subalpine larkspur** and **alpine groundsel** stand tall on steep slopes above Lake Ann in the Collegiate Peaks Wilderness. **Purple fringe** grows in small clusters around the shore of Trappers Lake in the Flat Tops Wilderness.

Purple penstemon grow in profusion on open slopes and meadows in the spring. Below Cheeseman Mountain penstemon thrive in a forest clear-cut west of Colorado Springs. The Colorado River cuts a serpentine path through solid sandstone below the penstemon-covered cliffs of Rattlesnake Canyon. The different flower colors are due to natural variation and lighting differences.

$\mathcal{T}$he steep slopes of Horseshoe Basin have large patches of **blue columbine**, **mountain bluebell**, and **lemon paintbrush**. The small turquoise-colored lake is in Ingram Basin above Telluride. Difficult lighting conditions of full shade and full sun can best be accommodated with a split filter, half clear and half dark. Overleaf: An almost unbelievable concentration of bright **red paintbrush** with some **arnica** and **lupine** in the mix. The unnamed summits are in the Maroon Bells–Snowmass Wilderness.

Silvery lupine along with **lemon** and **rosy paintbrush** combine in a tundra design in the Maroon Bells–Snowmass Wilderness. **Fireweed**, **trailing daisy** and **foxtail barley** create a delightful grouping north of Crested Butte.

𝓕og mixed with rocky tarns near timberline creates exotic conditions in the Gunnison National Forest south of Taylor Pass. **Drummond's rush**, **one-headed daisy**, **alpine buttercup**, and **elephant heads** grow to the waters edge, while **lemon paintbrush** appear like bright candles and share a rocky shelf with **bistort** and **alpine avens**.

*B*eautiful flowers and bright blue skies with distant mountains define Colorado. **Western wallflower** carpet an open field below the snow-covered Sangre de Cristos. **Alpine avens** congregate before a tundra tarn with the reflected image of Uncompahgre Peak, 14,309 feet, the highest summit in the San Juans.

$\mathcal{T}$wo photos with dramatic differences in elevation but with a similar rocky feeling. **Purple penstemon** occupy a craggy ledge in the narrows of the Big Thompson Canyon at 6,000 feet. **Mountain laurel**, a multi-branched shrub, grows over the boulders at the edge of Missouri Lake, 11,000 feet, in the Holy Cross Wilderness.

*𝒯wo examples of magical hazy-bright light, caused by a thin overcast diffusing the sunlight. A colorful moth soaks up the sun to dry its wings following an afternoon thunderstorm. The moth sits on **shrubby cinquefoil**, blending in with some dry flower blossoms. A small stream adds character to the mixture of **purple fringe** and **alpine wallflower** on the White River Plateau.*

*Overleaf: The contrast between distant meadow and mountain and foreground flowers excites the eye. The cliffside **paintbrush** add color to the Maroon Bells–Snowmass Wilderness while across the Crystal River canyon is Treasury Mountain, 13,462 feet, in the Raggeds Wilderness.*

$\mathcal{R}$ocks and flowers would seem to be a contradiction, but in fact the rocks aid the flowers by providing protection from harsh winds. At the left, violet **sky pilot**, **mountain bluebell** and **lemon paintbrush** decorate a north facing ridge, above timberline, in the Sawatch Range. Above, **silvery lupine** with a few **rosy paintbrush** adorn the tundra in the Elk Mountains.

45

*S*now and flowers would seem to go together like oil and water. However, it can snow above timberline at anytime of the year as these July and early-September photos show. **Elephant heads** wear a mantle of snow along the South Fork of Halfmoon Creek in the San Isabel National Forest. On the Continental Divide south of Lake City, a light dusting of snow coats the tundra surrounding **alpine sunflower** and **sky pilot**.

46

Flowers tend to congregate at the inflows and outflows of bodies of water. A large cluster of **rose crown** and lime green moss thrive at a mountainside seep which flows into Oliver Twist Lake along the crest of the Mosquito Range. **Parry primrose** grow in tall clusters along the outflow from a small lake in Ice Lake Basin.

$\mathcal{D}$istant high mountains, along with dense clusters of mixed flowers celebrate Colorado. So tight are the **alpine avens** and **mountain bluebell** that they would seem to want to fight. The San Juan Mountains can be seen in the distance with the Red Mountain group adding a dash of color. A somber mountain can be seen above Lower Halfmoon Lake with **blue columbine**, **alpine avens** and **lemon paintbrush** in the foreground.

If a flower has many slender petals in a flat disk around a large center, it is a member of the aster family. The color can be yellow, white or pink. Examples include sunflower, daisy, groundsel, senecio, arnica, and ragwort. The left photo shows **alpine sunflower**, **purple fringe** and **alpine clover** above timberline in the Lizard Head Wilderness. Above, **subalpine arnica**, **sticky geranium** and **rosy paintbrush** cover the tundra in the White River National Forest.

Overleaf: The snowcapped Medicine Bow Mountains are reflected in a small pool along Grass Creek in the Colorado State Forest. This gentle slope with seeping water supports a lush carpet of **homely buttercup***.*

$\mathscr{A}$bove Yule Lake in the Raggeds Wilderness a sunlit mixture of **rosy paintbrush**, **lousewort**, **sunloving aster**, and **rock ragwort** thrive behind sheltering spruce trees near timberline. The right photo shows **alpine clover** mixed with **paintbrush** below the shadowed summit of Teakettle Mountain in Yankee Boy Basin.

*M*ountain streams and beautiful flowers cause the eye to pause—can you hear the rushing water? **Heartleaf arnica**, **subalpine daisy**, **rosy paintbrush**, **bistort**, and **mountain bluebell** flourish above timberline in the San Juan Mountains. **Bitter cress** thrives in and along a rushing stream below Mosquito Pass in the Pike National Forest.

$\mathcal{S}$ilhouetted flowers and trees against sunlit mountains add depth to these scenes. **Columbine** blossoms are shown against the south slopes of Grays Peak. Like so many wax candles, **lousewort** seem to illuminate the foreground in the Maroon Bells–Snowmass Wilderness.

$\mathcal{R}$eflections of trees and mountains with foreground flowers enchant the eye. A mixture of **rosy paintbrush**, **elephant heads**, **bitter cress** and **groundsel** grace the Gunnison National Forest. The black headwall of American Basin contrasts with delicate **marsh marigold** in the San Juan Mountains.

Overcast light evenly illuminates foreground flowers. The volcanic chimney of Lizard Head, 13,113 feet, in the San Miguel Mountains, contrasts with cliffside **columbine**. Four-foot-tall **fireweed** glistens from an afternoon rain shower in the Castle Creek valley north of Ashcroft.

Overleaf: The well-named **alpine sunflower** faces the sun on a twelve-thousand foot mountain top in the Collegiate Peaks Wilderness. Across Castle Creek valley is a continuum of high peaks; from left to right are Castle Peak, 14,265 feet, Conundrum Peak, 14,022 feet, and Cathedral Peak, 13,943 feet.

The **yellow water lily** *is surprisingly plentiful throughout Colorado. They commonly grow at elevations around 11,000 feet in shallow ponds and lakes. These are floating on the surface of Lily Pad Lake in the White River National Forest. While* **marsh marigold** *do not float, they will grow in standing water.*

Flower Photography

Brightly colored flowers coupled with the grandeur of mountains attract people and their cameras. Flower photography involves two key elements: where to find flowers and photo techniques. To find flowers it helps to understand the purpose of the flower to the plant. Flowers only exist to transfer pollen between plants. Unlike plants which use the wind to distribute their pollen, flowering plants use bright colors and/or sweet smells to attract agents (flies, bees, or hummingbirds) to distribute pollen. In the case of mountain flowers, sweet smells are seldom present. Bright colors work best in the open where the agents can see them from afar. I remember once sitting on a rock on a steep mountainside with a yellow hat. The next thing I knew, I had a hummingbird hovering two feet from my head wondering how to get at the nectar.

The majority of the photos in this book were taken within 1000 feet of timberline or between 10,500 and 12,500 feet. You should be able to find locations all over Colorado that duplicate the conditions I found. Simply open the book to a photo you like, evaluate the

elevation and terrain and go to similar spots in the mountains near you. This should enable you to find striking flower locales.

Successful photography has three key components: light, equipment, and film. Of these, light is the most critical. Too

False forget-me-not grace the forest floor in the San Juan Mountains.

much light is frequently more a problem than too little.

Flower photography, unlike general scenic photography, is best suited to low contrast light. With flowers, bright sunny light will create either dark shadows or overexposed highlights. Shadows add drama to a scenic, whereas in flower photography these shadows often create objectionable dark areas. If you

compensate with increased exposure to fill in the shadowed areas, you will burn out the highlight detail of the flower petals. This condition is particularly true if you are photographing light colored flowers. Blue, red, or other dark colors can be successfully photographed with bright light, if you can avoid too much dark shadow area.

Perhaps the best light for flower photography is hazy-bright light. You will recognize hazy-bright light by the faint shadow it produces. Such light creates just enough shadow to produce edge definition but not burn out the flower details. If I had to choose a light preference order, I would choose hazy-bright, light overcast, heavy overcast, blue shadow, and finally bright sun. Blue shadow is the light in shaded areas under a clear blue sky. While easy to work with in terms of exposure, your film will pick up an objectionable blue cast. A warming filter (81A or equivalent) will help compensate.

As for camera equipment, I recommend a 35mm SLR, for two major reasons: depth-of-field and lack of parallax problems. Depth-of-field refers to the closest and furthest objects in focus. A desirable range would be two feet to infinity, possible with a 24mm lens at f/22. No medium or large format camera mounts a lens shorter than 45mm, almost twice the focal length and therefore twice the close focus distance of a 24mm. If your budget has limits, get a 28-85mm zoom on a modern autofocus SLR that computes depth-of-field. Lacking a computer, you will need to stick to a single focal length lens with a depth-of-field scale. Non-SLR's almost always come with a fixed lens of 35-45mm focal length, but they lack close focusing, and the viewing and picture taking optics are different, which causes parallax distortion. All of these terms are explained further in basic camera guides.

Because on a sunny day the f/22 aperture requires a shutter speed of 1/30th of a second and considerably slower on a cloudy day, we are in tripod country. Ninety-nine percent of all my photos are done on a tripod. For flower photos you will also need a tripod where the legs spread out almost flat, to get the camera closer to the ground.

A useful accessory is a collapsible reflector to direct light to shadow areas. Often this can save a high contrast scene. For filtration, I use a warming filter for blue shadow and a polarizing filter in sunny conditions. In addition to removing objectionable reflections from foliage, a polarizer will compress the dynamic range of the scene, thereby reducing the chance of burned out highlights. Their

Alpine fairy slipper grow among the **columbine** in Horseshoe Basin.

disadvantage is that on some films, some colors, notably greens, will shift to unacceptable hues.

When discussing film, the first question you need to ask is, what is the intended purpose of the photo? Only if you intend on publishing or want to project slides to an audience should you consider slide film. Color negative film is much faster, has more exposure latitude, and is less expensive than slide film. That said, every photo in this book was done on Fuji Velvia, ASA 50, fine grain, high contrast, color slide film. Your local supermarket or discount store will not carry this film, so don't bother asking. If you're determined to use slide film, I recommend a ±½ stop bracket around the nominal exposure.

We haven't discussed wind, the fickle breath of Mother Nature, which frustrates all flower photographers. I've tossed many perfectly exposed photos that are wind-blurred. Other than a tent or an assistant with a shield, I have few suggestions.

Experience is a great teacher, particularly if you make mental or written notes. Review your results and compare with your expectations and notes to develop a strategy for your next flower photo self-assignment. Good shooting!!!

Roger Edrinn

*Overleaf: An eroded volcanic canyon displays the striking rock colors of Yankee Boy Basin. The basin, renowned for its summer flowers, shows off its **Colorado columbine** and **alpine avens**.*